Welcoming Rama

Krishna's Mercy

Copyright © 2012 Krishna's Mercy

All rights reserved.

www.krishnasmercy.org
www.facebook.com/krishnasmercy

CONTENTS

Introduction i

Chapter 1 - A Transcendentalist's Checklist Part 1 3

Chapter 2 - A Transcendentalist's Checklist Part 2 ..13

Chapter 3 - Impetus For Action....................................23

Chapter 4 - Parallel Lines 32

Chapter 5 - Chief of the Gods 41

Chapter 6 - Comparing Ramayanas 50

Chapter 7 - The Imperishable Realm..........................60

Chapter 8 - Fruits of the Forest....................................68

Chapter 9 - Lost in Ignorance 76

INTRODUCTION

"Dearest Shabari, who to attain spiritual abode do strive,
Welcome Rama and His brother Lakshmana when they arrive."

A good disciple follows the guru's lead,
The instructions without question they heed.

So the female ascetic who lived near Pampa Lake,
Accepting counsel, best fruits of forest to take.

Offered them to Rama when the brothers to her place came,
Though just berries, were accepted as nectar all the same.

Never mind she was a woman living renounced,
For her devotion, Rama gave her stature pronounced.

CHAPTER 1 - A TRANSCENDENTALIST'S CHECKLIST PART 1

"Have you conquered all the obstacles in the way of your practice of austerities? Has your practice of austerity and penance steadily increased? O lady who possesses asceticism for wealth [tapodhane], have you been able to control your anger and your eating?" (Lord Rama speaking to Shabari, Valmiki Ramayana, Aranya Kand, 74.8)

By associating with devotees or reading the classic Vedic scriptures, one may ultimately decide to take up bhakti-yoga, or devotional service. The seeds of spirituality certainly can vary. Some are looking for ways to be more religious, while others are looking for that one thing that provides true happiness. Either way, simply taking the initial step and having a sincere desire for success are enough to guarantee the ultimate reward of practicing the ultimate spiritual discipline. But success doesn't necessarily come overnight. Having the desire for self-realization is certainly nice, but perfection only comes through steady practice. Along the way, it is nice to measure our progress to see how we are doing in relation to our end-goal. In this regard, it is nice to have a series of questions we can ask ourselves, a way to tell if we are on the right path or if we are headed in the wrong direction. Thankfully, Lord Rama, an incarnation of the Supreme Godhead, through a series of questions posed to the great female sage Shabari, gave us precisely the checklist we are looking for.

Before going any further, it would be helpful to perform a quick review of how progress is measured in other areas of life. For students, progress is measured through homework assignments, term papers, and examinations. The exams carry the most weight, so it is important to perform well on them. Exams are important not only for elementary school students, but also for adults in the real world. If a person wants to become a lawyer, doctor, or certified accountant, they must pass a series of examinations which are quite difficult. Moreover, many vocations require professionals to keep taking exams every few years or so in order to demonstrate their proficiency.

These exams consist of questions relating to the subject matter that the examinees are supposed to know. For example, doctors are asked questions pertaining to medicine, lawyers are asked questions pertaining to logic and established law, and accountants are tested on their ability to audit financial statements and their ability to apply tax laws in the appropriate circumstances. Not only are students supposed to know the answers to these questions, but they also must understand the underlying concepts and how to apply them. This is where the exams take on their difficulty. Passing an important exam isn't all about memorizing facts and regurgitating them on command.

In order to gauge progress in spiritual life, exams are also required. But who will administer these tests? In the Vedic tradition, the spiritual master, or guru, is very important. In fact, Lord Krishna Himself states that without approaching a spiritual master, there is no chance of success. This logically makes sense, for without taking instruction from a qualified teacher of a particular subject, we would be unable to learn anything. One may argue that you could just as easily learn medicine or law by reading books, but even this method involves submission to a higher authority. After all, the books didn't write themselves. Professors and other highly learned professionals of their field write these books for the benefit of future practitioners.

Vedic wisdom is best acquired through aural reception. The hearing process is the most effective for taking in any information; hence the Vedas were originally passed down through an oral tradition. The Vedas are also known as the shrutis, meaning that which is heard. Based on these facts, we can deduce that the best way to take up spiritual life is to hear from a spiritual master. In this past, young students would live at the gurukula, or the school run by the guru. In today's world, gurukulas are hard to find, thus making it more difficult to find a bona fide spiritual master who can teach us. Therefore less conventional means have to be adopted, such as approaching a guru by consulting their written instruction or recorded words. In reality, this method can be just as effective as personal contact, for there is no difference between a guru and their instructions.

So let's assume that we have approached a spiritual master by reading their books or listening to their recorded lectures. The most famous Vaishnava saint of the recent past is His Divine Grace A.C. Bhaktivedanta Swami Prabhupada. He authored over fifty books and left behind hours and hours of recorded lectures and speeches. One can focus exclusively on Prabhupada's teachings and have enough information to gain a perfect understanding of God and one's relationship to Him. Prabhupada's primary recommendation for aspiring transcendentalists was that they take up the process of regularly chanting God's names, "Hare Krishna Hare Krishna, Krishna Krishna, Hare Hare, Hare Rama Hare Rama, Rama Rama, Hare Hare". This is the most important recommendation, for it is the most effective process of devotional service. Chanting engages the tongue and ears in religious life. By chanting this mantra at least sixteen rounds a day on a set of japa beads, much of one's time becomes dedicated to serving Krishna. Along with this chanting routine, Prabhupada advised everyone to give up the four pillars of sinful life: meat eating, gambling, illicit sex, and intoxication.

Let's say that we take up devotional service, trying to adhere to these guidelines. How do we know if we are progressing? The scriptures give us a list of the qualities a devotee should possess, so naturally we can consult this list and see if we are developing these qualities. This is certainly one way to gauge our progress, but how do we know if we are on the right track? This is the most important barometer, for if we are headed in the wrong direction, our activities are essentially a waste of time. In order to help us in our service, Lord Rama, an incarnation of God, posed a series of questions to the highly exalted female sage Shabari. Though these questions were directed at Shabari, we can ask them of ourselves as well.

At the time Lord Rama was roaming the forests of India with His younger brother Lakshmana. The Vedas tell us that Krishna is God's original form, but that He expands Himself into various forms to perform activities on earth. Lord Rama was one such expansion, appearing as a handsome and pious prince of the Raghu dynasty. While living in the forest, Rama's wife, Sita Devi, was kidnapped by the Rakshasa demon Ravana. Rama and Lakshmana went searching for Sita and along the way they were advised to visit Shabari.

Immediately upon seeing Rama and Lakshmana, Shabari, who was quite advanced in age, approached the two brothers and touched their feet. This is quite noteworthy because according to social conventions, Rama and Lakshmana, who were young men at the time, were inferiors to Shabari. She knew that Rama was the Supreme Personality of Godhead, so she had no qualms about offering obeissances to Him. Acknowledging her humble attitude, the Lord kindly asked her a series of questions relating to her progress in spiritual life.

Lord Rama first asked Shabari if all hindrances to the performance of her asceticism were removed. Why is this important? In order to measure our progress, we have to see where we are in relation to the end-goal. In devotional service, which is the first class spiritual discipline, the end-goal is to go back to home, back to Godhead, after our current life is over. This end-goal relates to the current body, for the liberated soul actually never gives up service to the Lord even in the afterlife. The soul is imperishable, while the body is not. The body will eventually perish at the time of death, so the soul needs a place to go afterwards. Depending on our consciousness at the time of death, the soul either remains in the land of the perishable bodies, or it immediately ascends to the spiritual world, where it assumes an eternal spiritual body and associates with the Supreme Lord.

Getting a perishable body in the next life is not very difficult. We really don't have to do anything, just simply eat, sleep, mate, and defend, and we are sure to get a body in the next life which will be subject to birth, old age, disease, and death. In order to get a spiritual body, we must engage in spiritual activities, i.e. devotional service. Desiring to take up this activity and actually practicing it perfectly are two different things. Therefore it is important to remove all hindrances to our performance of devotional service. Since devotional life is the antithesis of material life, it can be considered a form of austerity, or tapah. In this way, Lord Rama's first question to Shabari related to her performance of tapasya. He was essentially asking her, "Are you able to perform your religious duties? Have you successfully removed obstacles that come your way?"

Applying these same questions to our own life, we should see whether or not we have anything holding us back from chanting our rounds. Is there any one thing in particular that is keeping us from chanting regularly? Is there anything that is holding us back from abandoning meat eating or drinking alcohol? If there are, we must remove these things as soon as possible. This may seem like an extreme step, but the more anarthas, or unwanted things, we can remove, the sooner we will see progress in spiritual life.

Lord Rama's next question was whether or not Shabari's asceticism was growing stronger day by day. This one issue is so important that it could fuel discussions for days and days. When people take up weightlifting or bodybuilding, they often keep a journal to track their progress. They want to make sure that they are lifting heavier and heavier weights as time goes on. Otherwise, what is the point to bodybuilding? By the same token, our eagerness for devotional service should increase day by day.

Otherwise, we are just going through the motions, or we are not engaging in our activities properly. Maybe there is something getting in our way and thus quelling our enthusiasm. Devotional service is all about love, so if our attachment to God is not steadily increasing, we aren't really progressing. Eagerness in religious practice is an easy metric to measure. We simply have to compare where we currently are in our spiritual practice verses where we were in the past. For example, if we are chanting less rounds today than we did in the past, we are obviously not progressing. Our asceticism is getting weaker, so we need to change things. If the opposite is true, we are surely on the right path.

Lord Rama's next two questions related to anger and eating habits. Anger is an emotion reserved for the weak. Anger doesn't really help us perform any meaningful activities since it takes away our ability to think clearly. Realizing God and understanding His glories requires sobriety on our part. Intoxication takes away our sobriety and so does anger. Anger is the result of lust, which is the result of uncontrolled passions. Religious life is part of the mode of material goodness and hopefully pure goodness as well. Being in the modes of goodness and pure goodness shield us from the effects of the mode of passion. If after taking up spiritual life, our anger is increasing, it means that the mode of passion must still be very strong. One's control over their anger is indicative of progress in spiritual life.

Lord Rama asked Shabari if she was able to control her eating. Diet is one of the most difficult things to control. The tongue is always telling us to eat this and that, even though we know that if we eat too much, we will suffer the effects later on. The best way to control our eating habits is to try to eat just enough food required for our satiation and food which is Krishna prasadam. Prasadam is sanctified food which has first been offered with love and devotion to Krishna. Since offering and eating prasadam are spiritual practices, they automatically keep one's eating habits regulated. In this way, taking stock of our eating habits represents yet another great way to judge our spiritual progress. If we are eating more today than we used to, or if we are unable to control the urges of the tongue, we likely need some more focus and dedication in our spiritual endeavors.

Since the end-goal is to have association with Krishna, the best way to measure spiritual progress is to see how much Krishna is in our life. During the course of the day, how often do we think of the Lord? How often do we say His name, and how often do we do something specifically for His benefit? A good family man is one who spends time with their family members, offering them service through financial and emotional support. In a similar manner, a good devotee is one who spends as much time with Krishna as possible. The Lord is Absolute, so there is no difference between His personal form, His names, or books which describe His glories. Shabari's darshana of Rama and Lakshmana indicates that her practice of devotional service, through dedication to austerity and penance, was perfect. If we remain steady on the virtuous path, and take stock of our progress at periodic intervals, we too can see the Supreme Lord.

CHAPTER 2 - A TRANSCENDENTALIST'S CHECKLIST PART 2

"Have you observed all the regulative principles and have you achieved happiness of mind? O lady who speaks beautifully, has your service to your guru been fruitful?" (Lord Rama speaking to Shabari, Valmiki Ramayana, Aranya Kand, 74.9)

The concept of a pocket guide is certainly nice. When discussing topics relevant to a certain discipline, one can find volumes upon volumes of written instruction and detailed guides with rules and regulations. Sometimes, however, we just want a quick summary which highlights the important aspects to a certain philosophy or discipline. These pocket guides are so named because they are small enough to fit inside of a pocket; thus allowing us to carry vital information with us wherever we go. If we keep something in our pocket, we can reference it at any time. This is one of the reasons why cellular phones are so popular. In an instant, we can talk to our friends, check our email, check the weather, take pictures, and even listen to music. If pocket guides can be helpful to us in areas relating to material life, they most certainly can prove to be even more beneficial when they focus on spiritual matters. But where can we find such a guide?

The Ten Commandments of the Christian Bible seem like the most streamlined guide, a quick-start introduction into religion. While the Ten Commandments give us the basic rule-set of do's and don'ts, daily life involves activity. At any given time, we must be doing something. Though most of us initially believe that the ultimate achievement in life is to get out of doing work, i.e. acquire enough money so that we can sit and relax, we see that even the well-off are victims of distress. Even if all of our basic necessities are covered and we don't have to work for a living, we still must perform action. Activity is the essence of life, serving as the key distinction between a living body and a dead one. Since we all must perform activity, the Vedas, which are the original scriptures for all of mankind, advise that we direct our activities towards the proper goal, i.e. that of understanding God.

Learning about God, understanding who He is, what He looks like, and what our relationship to Him is makes up the discipline known as spirituality. Religion is similar except that it often delves into organized establishments and legislative edicts. The Vedas tell us that spirituality is really an occupational duty, something which is eternal and that is never meant to be abandoned. Hence the Vedas refer to spiritual life as sanatana-dharma, or the eternal occupation of the soul. So we have the Ten Commandments and we also have this idea of activity, but where do we go from here? What if we don't have the time to read every volume of religious scripture that exists? Where can we go to get a pocket guide, a quick-start summary of what steps need to be taken to be successful in spiritual life? Luckily for us, the Supreme Lord has often discussed these issues in the past with His great devotees. Due to the causeless mercy of the great saints who recorded these conversations in written form, we can easily consult these teachings and make our lives perfect as a result.

The Supreme Absolute Truth, the eternally existing Personality of Godhead, appeared on earth in human form many thousands of years ago as the handsome prince of Ayodhya named Rama. As part of His pastimes, Lord Rama travelled through the forests of India, visiting great sages along the way. Lord Rama appeared in the guise of a man, but He was really an incarnation of Lord Narayana, who is the four-handed form of God residing in the spiritual world. The word nara refers to a man or human being, and thus Narayana means the source of all naras, or persons. Since man is made after God, the Lord is the original source. When the Lord descends from the spiritual world, His spiritual form is known as an avatara, or one who descends. An avatara is completely spiritual in nature and not a product of maya. Sometimes the avatara, or deity representation of the same, is referred to as the saguna form, meaning God with attributes. This description is based on the perspective of the conditioned living entity. The Lord appears in the guise of a human being, but He is never tainted by any gunas, or material qualities. It is similar to how we refer to the sun as setting and rising, when in reality it never moves. The sun's properties never change, and similarly, the Supreme Lord always retains a spiritual body. There is a class of transcendentalists known as Mayavadis, who take everything to be maya, or illusory material nature. Maya means that which is not, hence maya is taken to be an illusory energy which is not God. The word vada means conclusion, thus the Mayavadis are those whose ultimate conclusion is that everything in this world is maya, including the avataras of Vishnu and Their deity representations.

In reality, anything pertaining exclusively to material nature is certainly maya, but there is a higher energy which is ever-existing and unchangeable. This is the spiritual energy, and since it is eternal, it cannot be classified as maya, or false. We living entities are actually part of the spiritual energy, but since we are currently covered by a body made up of maya, we are clouded by illusion. When the Supreme Lord descends to this world, however, His body is not made up of material elements. Since the Lord is the source of everything, there is no difference between His spirit and body. Even His body is spiritual, or ever existing. Since He is superior to us, and since He is also the reservoir of pleasure, it is our duty to worship Him.

During Lord Rama's time, those seeking spiritual enlightenment took refuge in the forests. The wilderness is much more peaceful, and life there is very simple. For a renounced sage, meals are taken care of by eating whatever fruits fall from the trees and whatever roots are on the ground. Bathing and drinking water can be taken from the nearby rivers and lakes, and housing can be found either in a cave or by erecting a small thatched hut. Since life is so simple, there is more time for performing religious rituals, adhering to austerities, and contemplating on the Supreme. When we speak of contemplation, we are not referring to the conjuring up of images by the mind. The Supreme Lord is ever-existing, and though He has multitudes of forms, none of His features or attributes can be concocted by man. Rather, the Supreme Lord has been kind enough to grant the spiritual vision with which to see Him to several exalted devotees of the past. These great saints then recorded what they saw in authorized books such as the Ramayana, Mahabharata, and Puranas. Thus when sages contemplate on the Supreme Lord, they remember an eternally existing form such as Lord Krishna, Narayana, Rama, etc.

In the Treta Yuga, many sages had the extraordinary benediction of getting to meet Rama face to face. One such fortunate soul was the female sage Shabari. Lord Rama and His younger brother, Lakshmana, were roaming the forests at the time looking for Rama's wife, Sita, who had just been kidnapped. Being advised to visit Shabari's hermitage, Rama and Lakshmana made their way to her dwelling. When Shabari saw the two brothers approaching, she immediately greeted them by touching their feet and welcoming them. Shabari was no fool after all. She knew who Lord Rama was, for she had been told on a previous occasion that she would be granted liberation from the cycle of birth and death upon meeting the Lord. According to standard etiquette, Shabari was a superior since she was a sage and also much older than Rama and

Lakshmana, who were both members of the warrior caste. Yet since she knew of Rama's divinity, Shabari was the one who offered obeisances.

How did Lord Rama repay her kindness? Normally when we visit a friend or family member, we'll ask them how things are going and if anything's new. Rama, however, knew that Shabari was a dedicated sage and that she was very pious. Keeping this in mind, Rama asked her questions pertaining to her religious practices. In the above referenced statement, we see that Rama is asking Shabari if she is able to successfully complete her vows, if she is happy in her service, and if she has gotten the full benefit out of serving her spiritual master. These three questions serve as a great pocket guide for us to hold on to. If we simply ask these questions of ourselves on a daily basis, we are sure to always remain on the virtuous path.

Let's review the first part of Shri Rama's initial question. The Lord asked Shabari if she was able to successfully observe her niyamah, or regulative principles.. The importance of this is quite obvious. Finish what you start. Finishing a job to its completion is considered beneficial. We take up a new project precisely so that we can finish it and enjoy the resulting rewards. It is the desire for these rewards that serves as the impetus for our actions. If we don't finish our tasks, then the rewards don't come, and our actions end up being a waste of time. Spiritual life is especially difficult due to the effects of material nature. For aspiring devotees, one of the requirements is that they should chant a set number of rounds on their japa beads every day. In this age especially, devotees are asked to chant the maha-mantra, "Hare Krishna Hare Krishna, Krishna Krishna, Hare Hare, Hare Rama Hare Rama, Rama Rama, Hare Hare", at least sixteen rounds a day. Agreeing to chant a set number of rounds each day is known as a vow. So if we vow to perform this activity, we should make sure to see it to its conclusion.

If we vow to abide by a certain regulative principle and then fail to carry out on our promise, what is the result? First off, we will feel like failures. Success undoubtedly brings confidence, and it lets us know that we can handle difficult tasks in the future. Failure takes us in the opposite direction. If we vow to do something and then renege, we don't gain any confidence. Confidence is required in spiritual life; otherwise success will never come. This is why Lord Rama posed this question to Shabari. The Lord knew that if she wasn't successfully abiding by her avowed regulative principles, she wasn't getting the full benefit of spiritual life.

The second part of Rama's first question pertained to the satisfaction felt by Shabari. Lord Rama wanted to know if she was satisfied by performing her vows; was her mind at ease? This is also another barometer of progress in spiritual life. Lord Rama is always seen smiling, for His face is beautiful and He gives pleasure to everyone He meets. Lord Krishna, the original form of God, is known as Shyamasundra, meaning the beautiful one who has the complexion of a dark raincloud. Associating with Krishna should most definitely bring about bliss and peace of mind. In fact, devotional service is the only way to achieve peace. In this instance, Rama is asking Shabari if her mind was satisfied and at ease, because if a devotee's mind is not at ease, there must be a problem. The source of the problem can be one's own mind and body, divine nature, or other living entities. Lord Rama wanted to know if she was in any trouble, because if she was, the Lord would most certainly take care of the problem. One of Krishna's names is Hari, which means one who removes distress. The Lord is so nice that if He sees His devotees being bothered, He will personally intervene to remedy the situation.

The last question asked by Rama is probably the most important. The Lord asked Shabari if her service to her spiritual master had borne fruit. This is the key to success in spiritual life. We must find a devotee of Krishna who has seen the Truth, who practices the regulative principles, whose mind is always at ease, and who only has Krishna's interests at heart. After finding such a person, we must humbly submit ourselves to them and agree to follow their instructions. It is certainly ideal to find a guru and offer them service personally, but real submission comes through carrying out the orders of the spiritual master. There is no difference between a spiritual master and their teachings, or vani. Agreeing to wholeheartedly abide by the guru's instructions represents real submission.

What are the results of approaching a spiritual master and taking their instructions to heart? The creeper of devotional service gradually turns into a full blown tree, spurring branches of endless love and leaves of ecstatic emotion directed at the Supreme Lord. This is why Lord Rama asked Shabari if her service to her guru had brought about fruits, or saphala. If we submit to a bona fide spiritual master and humbly serve them by following their instructions, we will surely realize these fruits, which are the sweetest tasting rewards one could ask for. If we don't see the creeper of devotional service developing into something bigger, then it must mean that we have neglected to follow the guru's instructions or that we have approached the wrong spiritual master.

The beauty of this conversation is that Lord Rama didn't even need to ask these questions. He knew of Shabari's nature beforehand, but the Lord asked these questions anyway for her benefit. When devotees engage in devotional service, they are very enthusiastic. It is not that they want to show off, but they are very eager to discuss religious topics with others. Moreover, they cherish every opportunity they get to praise their spiritual master. Lord Rama asked these questions because He knew Shabari was eager to answer them.

We can take these questions posed by Rama as our pocket guide for measuring our progress in devotional service. By consulting these questions regularly, not only do we get to measure our progress in spiritual life, but we also get to associate with Lord Rama. Our goal in life should be to fix ourselves up to the point that if God should one day come to us and ask these same questions, we would be able to answer them with the same confidence and enthusiasm as Shabari did.

CHAPTER 3 - IMPETUS FOR ACTION

"Today, being graced with Your presence, I have obtained the results of my penances and austerities. Today, my birth has been made fruitful and my spiritual masters have been well honored." (Shabari speaking to Lord Rama, Valmiki Ramayana, Aranya Kand, 74.11)

Though many of the activities we perform on a daily basis are simply part of our routine, if we were to delve into the origins of such actions, we would find that they all have one thing in common. No matter the task, large or small, complicated or simple, the impetus for all action is the hope for some type of future enjoyment. This conclusion seems obvious enough, for why would we work hard unless there was some benefit to be derived from such effort? This same concept holds true with spiritual life, and unlike with our ordinary endeavors, when spirituality is practiced perfectly, it can bestow the highest of rewards, as it did to the famous female sage, Shabari, many thousands of years ago.

Let's first review what kinds of enjoyment we expect to receive from some of our more common activities. In this advanced technological age, one of the more popular forms of entertainment, especially for young men, is the playing of video games. Sports heroes can be seen performing their magic on television. When these athletes are successful, they hoist up the championship trophy and get all the glory. These victories don't come easy, as there is fierce competition between other professionals in their field. For the average person, winning Wimbledon or holding up the Stanley Cup is a mere pipe dream, something that will never be experienced.

Fear not, however, as there is a way to imitate these activities, a way to give the average person a watered down sense of enjoyment and bliss. Video games allow us to pretend to play some of the most difficult sports right in our very own living rooms. Through the use of televisions and gaming consoles, we can pretend to be Tiger Woods or Wayne Gretzky. Many of these games allow us to simulate an entire season of a particular sport. We can also participate in major tournaments such as the Masters, Wimbledon, the World Cup, etc. Competition is provided by either the computer, which is powered by artificial intelligence, or other human players. We can play with our friends and family at home or with strangers on the internet. The possibilities are endless.

Video games are popular because, as with any other activity, there is a desired end-result, a type of enjoyment that the player inherently expects to derive from the game. For example, if we play a Tiger Woods golf game, we obviously hope to gain proficiency over the controls. Our desire is to compete against other players and win tournaments. In this way, the expectation is to experience the thrill of victory, while hopefully avoiding the agony of defeat.

To those unfamiliar with gaming consoles, playing video games may seem like a waste of time. "Why are they pretending to do something when they can go outside and play the real thing? What are they getting out of playing these games? Do they really feel happy after beating their friend in a silly computer game?" The reality is that video game players most certainly do feel some sort of enjoyment from playing, otherwise why would they even take the time to play? This same concept actually applies to all of our activities. Even the things that we don't like to do, such as taking out the trash, washing the dishes, doing laundry, etc., are all performed with a desired positive result in mind. By performing our chores, we will hopefully feel happier knowing that our life is in order and that we're not living like slobs. Going to work on time and keeping up with our studies have similar built-in positive results.

While these facts seem pretty obvious to most of us, they are often overlooked with respect to spiritual life. Religion is seen as the polar opposite of fun. This stigma is the result of the perceived restrictive nature of religion. Spirituality is seen as a discipline full of rules and regulations that must be followed. If one violates these rules, they will have to deal with chastisement from religious leaders and other authority figures. None of us enjoy being yelled at or taken to task for our shortcomings, so why would we even want to associate with religion?

Yet just as with any other activity, transcendentalists take to spirituality with an intended goal in mind. The skeptic may say, "Yes, I know. They want to go to heaven. But heaven can only be achieved after death, meaning that a person must deprive themselves of fun for an entire lifetime. And even then, they aren't guaranteed of going to heaven." For the neophyte spiritualist, ascending to heaven after death is surely the desired goal. With this aim in mind, people take to various pious activities such as attending church, performing rituals in the home, and worshiping elevated religious personalities.

While wanting to go to heaven is certainly a nice goal, there is actually a much greater reward available to those who practice spirituality perfectly. The Vedas define religion as dharma, or one's occupational duty. If we equate dharma with the idea of ascending to heaven, it would mean that it is our duty to act in such a way so as to facilitate our ascension to the heavenly realm after death. Though going to heaven is a great reward, something which gives us enjoyment, how can the achievement of this reward be our dharma? What if we don't want to go to heaven? What if we're happy where we are right now?

Though going to heaven is certainly a nice reward, it should not be the main impetus for religious activity. The Vedas refer to religion as our occupational duty because our identity comes from the soul within. What does this mean? Currently we base our identity off of our bodily features. If we are born in America, we naturally identify ourselves as American. If our parents practice the Hindu faith, we will identify ourselves as Hindu, and so forth. These identifications are certainly valid within the scope of discussing nationality or religious affiliation, but our identities carry much greater importance than simply the geographic location of our birth or the religious practices of our ancestors.

Lord Krishna, the originator of Vedic wisdom, the Supreme Divine being, tells us that the soul is eternal. This means we are eternal; we have never taken birth nor have we ever died. The body certainly goes through birth, old age, disease, and death, but the soul does not. As a result, any identification made off bodily traits will be invalid in the grand scheme of things. We may be born as Americans in this life, but since the soul is eternal, it stands to reason that we may take birth in a different land in our next life. Since the soul doesn't change, neither does our identity. Therefore it is silly to identify ourselves based on the traits of our current body.

Since the soul is eternal, it must have an ever-existing quality, a set of activities which it is inclined to perform that provides enjoyment. This is where dharma comes into play. Dharma is an occupational duty, and it is sanatana, or eternal. When we practice dharma, we aren't looking for any type of material enjoyment or the alleviation of some sort of distress. Dharma is an eternal occupation because it is the inherent nature of the soul to derive transcendental pleasure through association with other souls. Currently our soul is covered up by a material dress, so when we interact with other living entities, we are only associating with their material coverings. For the soul to derive pleasure, it must associate with other souls, and more specifically, it must associate with those things which are free from the contaminations of matter.

In the body of every living entity, there reside two souls: the individual [atma] and the Super [Paramatma]. Paramatma represents God's expansion as an impartial witness who lives inside the heart for our benefit. Dharma is meant for connecting with this Supersoul. Unlike the atma which can transmigrate through various forms of bodies under the dictates of nature, the Supersoul is not subject to the same influences. This should make sense as the Supersoul is a manifestation of God and is thus the creator and controller of nature. The highest spiritual discipline is that which aims to associate with the Supersoul, to please it, and to take direction from it.

As we see with our normal activities, the impetus for action comes from the desire for rewards. In a similar manner, our soul is naturally inclined to performing spiritual activities, for the rewards achieved from spiritual association far surpass those we get from any other activity. Hence we see the real reason for taking to religious life. The Vedas tell us that this discipline of connecting our soul with the Supersoul is known as yoga. There are various kinds of yoga which all serve as stepping stones to achieving the end-goal of pure love for God. This is the real benefit of acting in accordance with dharma. Love for God is known as Krishna-prema, and it is the most pure form of affection that exists. If we adjust our activities in such a way that we achieve Krishna-prema, we'll know that our spiritual endeavors have borne fruit. This was the case with the great female sage Shabari.

God lives within as the Supersoul, but this soul is simply an expansion that emanates from the original person. Most of us refer to this original person as God, but the Vedas tell us that He has a more descriptive name: Krishna. Krishna means one who is all-attractive, and thus it is an appropriate way to address the Supreme Lord. Krishna has multitudes of forms, all of which serve different purposes. In His expansion as Lord Rama, God came to earth to protect the pious and grant them the wonderful benediction of seeing Him face to face. Many great personalities had the good fortune of meeting Rama, with Shabari being one of them. As part of His pastimes, Lord Rama travelled through the forests of India, living as a recluse, accompanied by His wife Sita Devi and younger brother Lakshmana.

On one unfortunate occasion, Sita was kidnapped by a Rakshasa demon. When Rama and Lakshmana went looking for her, they were told to pass by an area where a female ascetic lived. When we speak of God's pastimes, we must keep in mind that everything occurs for a reason. Nothing happens by chance. Rama's meeting with Shabari serves as a great illustration for this point. On a previous occasion, Shabari was granted the benediction that she would achieve liberation from the cycle of birth and death by having darshana, or a vision, of Lord

Rama. To make this prophecy hold true, as well as many other curses and predictions, God has to manipulate events in just the right way. Thus by Sita being kidnapped, the Lord was able to travel through the forests with Lakshmana and meet just the right people and grant benedictions to them.

When Rama and Lakshmana arrived at Shabari's hermitage, she immediately got up and touched their feet. Lord Rama then politely posed several questions to her relating to her ascetic vows. Rama wanted to know if she was progressing in spiritual life and if she was deriving the full benefit of her pious deeds. In the above referenced quote, Shabari is answering Rama's questions. We see that right off the bat, she lets Rama know that just by seeing Him in person all her pious deeds have borne fruit. This one statement speaks volumes, for it illustrates the essence of devotional service, or bhakti-yoga.

In the beginning stages we may take up devotional service to the Lord for various personal reasons. Maybe we are distressed, we want money, or we're inquisitive. The wise, however, take to devotional service because they want to know the Absolute Truth. What better way is there to know God than by seeing Him face to face? Shabari knew that since she saw Rama, there was no other conclusion to be reached. Whatever she had done in the past, whatever she had learned from her spiritual guides, must have all been worthwhile and correct, for she was now seeing God in front of her.

We too can be granted the same benediction. We shouldn't think that this event was an anomaly or something that can't happen for us. If we're sincere in our service, and if we kindly follow the instructions of fellow devotees, we will surely one day meet God. The other point to note here is that Shabari mentioned that by meeting Rama, her birth was blessed. According to the material estimation, being born as a vaishya [merchant], shudra [laborer], or woman is considered to be a second-class birth. But we see from Shabari's example that devotional service is open to every single person, regardless of the circumstances of their birth. Not only is devotional service open to everyone, but so are the resulting rewards, i.e. association with God.

So let us all take up the sublime engagement, devotional service to the Lord. Dharma exists eternally, so God is waiting for us to rekindle our relationship with Him. We don't need to take to spiritual life out of fear or frustration. Association with God represents the greatest reward in life, thus making devotional service the highest engagement. This fact alone should be enough to get us to turn our eyes towards Krishna. If we even get one look at the face of the Supreme Lord, we'll never want to turn away.

CHAPTER 4 - PARALLEL LINES

"Today, being graced with Your presence, I have obtained the results of my penances and austerities. Today, my birth has been made fruitful and my spiritual masters have been well honored." (Shabari speaking to Lord Rama, Valmiki Ramayana, Aranya Kand, 74.11)

Service paid to the spiritual master and worship of the Supreme Personality of Godhead run on parallel lines. By worshiping both parties simultaneously, one achieves the greatest reward of liberation from the repeated suffering brought on by contact with the temporary world. Only in the afterlife, the realm where spirituality reigns supreme, can the agonies brought on by gain, loss, birth, death, happiness, and sadness be permanently eradicated. In order to enter this realm, one must be stripped of all egoism and false pride. One must be a complete adherent to the dictates of the Divine Being, whose instructions are carried out in this world by His purified servants, the spiritual masters who embody virtue, kindness, compassion, and deference to the laws of the Supreme Master. While service to the guru brings pleasure to the Supreme Lord, the reciprocal benedictions bestowed on the sincere servant by God also bring pleasure to the spiritual master. This truth was stressed by the exalted female sage Shabari when she had the wonderful opportunity to meet the Supreme Personality of Godhead face to face.

In the world of sports, politics, literature, or any field which has achievements and accomplishments, there are often discussions pertaining to which person or team is the greatest of all time. The purpose behind such discussions is quite easy to decipher. Fans of sports, politics, and literature have particular favorite personalities, "stars of the game" if you will. In order to praise the stars, fans need a frame of reference, something or someone to compare achievements to. By having this juxtaposition, one is better able to offer a proper compliment to their particular favored party. For example, Sita Devi, the wife of Lord Rama, once offered a very nice compliment to her husband, Shri Rama, by making a comparison to a notable powerful entity.

"*O Raghava, if I am in Your company, even Shakra [Indra], the lord of the demigods, with his great strength would not be able to overpower me.*" (Sita Devi speaking to Lord Rama, Valmiki Ramayana, Ayodhya Kand, 29.6)

Lord Rama, an expansion of the original, all-blissful, ever-existing Personality of Godhead, roamed this earth many thousands of years ago in the guise of a pious, kshatriya prince. We can think of a kshatriya as the most honest and capable defender of the innocent. This honesty and dedication to righteousness doesn't exist only in theory. Rather, there are many occasions when a defender is put to the test. As the saying goes, "When the going gets tough, the tough get going", Shri Rama proved His mettle on many occasions, the most notable of which related to His exile from His opulent kingdom of Ayodhya.

When Rama was still a young man, He was on the precipice of coronation; He was to succeed His father on the royal throne. Yet through a series of unfortunate events, the kingdom was snatched away from Him at the last moment. To make matters worse, He was ordered to leave the community and not return for fourteen years, during which time He would have no ties to the regal life. God is atmarama, meaning one who is self-satisfied, so such an order didn't phase Shri Rama one bit. But He was married at the time, and as is custom in a marriage, the husband often has to deliver unpalatable news to the wife. A married man can't just stay out late all the time without telling his wife first. A good husband will not leave home without at least telling someone where they are going.

When Rama went to tell Sita the news, she didn't take to it too well. She wasn't necessarily worried about her future as queen being in jeopardy. Rather, she was dreading the impending separation from Rama. Instead of agreeing to her husband's request that she remain in the kingdom, Sita insisted on coming along. Her main argument was that, as Rama's shadow, it would be impossible for Him to roam the earth without her. In order for a shadow to exist, there must be an original light. In this way, Sita was saying that she couldn't exist without the beacon of light which was her husband.

In order to convince Rama of her position, Sita pointed to His extraordinary abilities in the area of defense. Rama tried to dissuade Sita from going by reminding her of the dangers of forest life. Sita not only countered this argument by saying that Rama was strong, but she emphatically pointed out that not even Indra, the king of the heavenly planets, could harm her if she was in Rama's company. Comparisons to Indra are quite commonplace in Vedic literature. He is the strongest of the suras, or the devoted living entities possessing heavenly bodies. Therefore if someone is stronger than Indra, it means that they must be one of the most capable fighters in the universe.

When praising an athlete or famous figure, one will often make comparisons to legends of the past. Every sport or discipline of interest has a specific icon, or standard bearer, for the sport. In ice hockey, the icon is Wayne Gretzky, in basketball Michael Jordan, in computers Bill Gates. If a new player comes along and breaks established records, comparisons will be made to the previous legends. If a player should happen to surpass a former great's achievements, debates will begin as to which person is the greatest of all time.

What often gets overlooked in this debate is the influence of the legend on the newcomer. Let's take Wayne Gretzky for example. Prior to Gretzky's arrival in the National Hockey League, Gordie Howe was considered the greatest player of all time. Gretzky was actually a big fan of Howe growing up, so it would stand to reason that Howe had a significant influence on Gretzky's career. So when Wayne amassed wonderful point totals and goals, shouldn't Howe have been given some of the credit? If the predecessors are somewhat responsible for the achievements of the newer generation, doesn't the "greatest of all time" argument lose its steam? How can someone be the greatest of all time if previous greats were partially responsible for their abilities?

This speaks to the truth that our teachers and role models make us who we are. In the Vedic tradition, the first objects of worship are the parents. They take care of us in the early years of life and give us a basic understanding of right and wrong. In the absence of this care and affection, we easily could be led off the straightened path. In adulthood, the object of worship is the guru, or spiritual master. The parents give us our first birth, but in order to achieve success in a spiritual sense, we need a second birth. The spiritual master gives us this reawakening of divine consciousness through the initiation process. When one is properly educated in a spiritual sense, they no longer see bodily designations; they see only spirit and its relationship to an ever-changing matter.

Not only do students learn about spirituality from their gurus, but they also become familiar with the most sublime engagement of devotional service, or the religion of love. The aim of life is to change one's consciousness to the point where all thoughts are revolving around love, service, and affection for the Supreme Spirit. This Divine Personality goes by different names according to time and circumstance, but the Vedas inform us that His most complete name and form is Krishna, a word which means all-attractive. Devotional service aims to keep one's mind always fixed at the lotus feet of the Supreme Lord, who possesses a love-evoking, transcendental form.

A spiritual master is not chosen on a whim, but rather is sought out based on their qualifications. Of all the characteristics of a guru, his most endearing qualification is his ability to liberate his disciples from the repeated cycle of birth and death. If our consciousness is not purified by the time we die, we will be forced to take birth again to a new set of parents and repeat the same knowledge-acquiring process. If we can find a bona fide spiritual master and follow their instructions wholeheartedly, we can avoid this unnecessary rebirth.

Since the guru is a representative of Krishna, he is to be honored in the same way that one would worship the Lord. This means that if we fall flat on the floor and offer our obeisances to the spiritual master, we are essentially offering our prayers to the Supreme Lord. The spiritual master is often compared to a boatman who carries the wayward spirit soul across the ocean of nescience back to the transcendental realm. In this way, we see that service to the guru equates to happiness to the Supreme Lord. Krishna is happy because the guru is bringing back one of His lost souls, an expansion of the Supreme Energetic which is meant to provide enjoyment to the Supreme Enjoyer.

By satisfying the guru with our service, the chain of causation eventually finds its way back to God. When the guru is pleased, the guru's guru is pleased, the guru's guru's guru is satisfied, and so on. What's often overlooked, however, is the end-result of such service and its effect on the parties involved. We know what the initial act of service to the guru will lead to, but what effect does the result of this action bring? For example, say that we please Krishna by pleasing the guru. If the Lord offers us a nice benediction in return, are we the only ones benefitted? According to the opinion of the most exalted associates of the Lord, those liberated souls who properly served their gurus, the benedictions received from God directly affect the same chain of spiritual masters. This fact was reiterated by the female sage Shabari.

Rama's younger brother Lakshmana also insisted on accompanying the Lord during His travels through the forest. Agreeing to take Sita and Lakshmana with Him, Rama embarked on His journey. On one unfortunate occasion, Sita would be kidnapped by a Rakshasa demon. In their subsequent search for her whereabouts, Rama and Lakshmana made their way to the hermitage of Shabari. When she saw them approaching, she immediately got up and touched their feet. She had been waiting for Rama ever since her spiritual guides told her that she would be granted liberation upon meeting the Lord. After being welcomed in such a hospitable way, Rama asked Shabari some very nice questions pertaining to her spiritual practices. One of the questions He asked was whether or not her service to her gurus had borne fruit.

In the above referenced statement, Shabari is responding to Rama's questions. We see that she states that the service she offered to her guravah, her spiritual masters and respectable elders, has most certainly borne fruit. She not only stipulates that the service was successful, but she also provides a reason. Shabari states that by having Rama's darshana, seeing Him face to face, her gurus have been duly honored. This speaks to the truth that the spiritual master and the Supreme Lord are always linked. You cannot serve one and neglect the other. No one is dearer to Krishna than His sincere servant.

Shabari's kind words also reinforce the fact that a person's greatness and accomplishments are a reflection on their teachers. By meeting Rama, which is the highest benediction one can achieve in life, Shabari honored herself and her spiritual masters. After all, it was her gurus who taught her about spiritual life and how to perform tapasya. They taught her how to control her anger and her eating habits. Not only Shabari, but every one of us has to be taught how to live a regulated life. In the absence of this instruction, we would most certainly take to nefarious behavior or those activities which would end up harming us.

This event with Shabari took place many thousands of years ago during the Treta Yuga, but we see that even back then women were eligible for spiritual instruction. Even though it wasn't common for women to take to an ascetic lifestyle, those who were properly qualified certainly could. The guru's mercy is open to every single person, so anyone who is sincerely interested in spiritual life should try to humbly soak in the kind instructions of the pure devotee. Though we can never properly repay the debts we owe to the great saints of the past, if the Supreme Lord should happen to be pleased with us, all of our teachers and superiors would be duly honored at the same time, thus completing the circle.

CHAPTER 5 - CHIEF OF THE GODS

"O best of men, today, by worshiping You - Rama who is the greatest of all the gods - my religious practices have become fruitful and my ascension to the heavenly realm will surely take place." (Shabari speaking to Lord Rama, Valmiki Ramayana, Aranya Kand, 74.12)

Herein we get one of the most concise descriptions about spiritual life and what is needed for success. There are many religious systems, or dharmas, that people adopt over the course of their many lifetimes on earth, but there is one method of worship, and also one object of worship, that stands head and shoulders above all others. Those who worship Lord Krishna, or one of His Vishnu expansions such as Lord Narayana or Rama, achieve all the opulences and benedictions available to those who practice other religious systems. Not only is Narayana the chief among the gods, but the rewards bestowed to His devotees are also foremost.

Why would we want rewards from God? Activity is sparked by personal interest. Unless there is something in it for us, why would we take to a particular activity? Even acts of charity and general altruism have personal motives built into them. "I will give in charity so that one day they can find a cure to cancer or other deadly disease. I will help the downtrodden so that their suffering will end. In this way, I will feel better and so will the recipients of my charity." Even this perceived unselfishness has a hidden agenda behind it. By the same token, spiritualists also look for personal benefits. The driving force to all activity is the potential for enjoyment.

Enjoyment has two aspects to it. The first part involves the removal of distresses. The Vedas tell us that all miseries in life come from one of three sources. Adhibhautika miseries come from other living entities. Bhautika refers to bhuta, which means a living entity. These miseries are easy to identify. We run into someone during the day that is mean to us, or maybe we see another person that wants to steal our possessions. In extreme cases there is war, government tyranny, or oppression. These are all adhibhautika miseries. The second kind of misery is that which comes from our own body and mind; hence it is referred to as adhyatmika. Adhyamta refers to the soul, the spirit inside of us which causes all of our activities. Every action we perform has a commensurate reaction; hence we feel either happy or sad depending on the nature of the result. Our own body can cause us great grief, either through diseases or through mental agony. If the love of our life suddenly leaves us or if we don't do well on a test, the resulting sadness is very difficult to overcome. The third kind of misery is that which comes about from Mother Nature. Earthquakes, hurricanes, floods, etc. are all part of nature's workings. The Vedas refer to these miseries as Adhidaivika. This nature has some intelligence behind it though.

The word "adhidaivika" means that which comes from daiva, or the divine. Daiva is derived from the word deva, which means a god or a celestial being. The common misconception associated with Hinduism is that it involves many gods. This is indeed true, but at the same time, it is misleading. There are many devas, but there is only one chief God, or Supreme Personality of Godhead. If there is one God, why are there so many devas? This brings us back to the issue of enjoyment. We experience varieties of enjoyment and happiness in this world, but actually there is a place where the level of enjoyment is much higher. Enjoyment involves the removal of distress and also an object from which one derives pleasure. Normally these objects are of the material variety: clothes, jewels, money, sex life, etc. We see these objects in our everyday life, but they all actually originate elsewhere. We can think of life on earth as a reflection of something that exists in the real form somewhere else. That somewhere is heaven, the planetary system above ours.

The devas reside in heaven. They live a much more opulent lifestyle than we do. Devas also live for much longer than we do. The original deva, the first created living entity, is Lord Brahma. He lives for billions and billions of years. He is the oldest person in the world and his associates are also very old. Since they are elevated living entities, the devas, who are also known as demigods, reside on heavenly planets where there is an abundance of gold, women, jewels, and other opulences. Heaven exists for those who are interested in advanced material enjoyment. Ascension to heaven isn't easy, for it requires the performance of many great sacrifices, or yajnas, and adherence to piety.

The desire to ascend to heaven is quite natural. The threefold miseries of life can get to be too much for us after a while. We want a way out, a place to go where we won't have to feel miserable anymore. In addition, we'd like to have a place where life can be enjoyed to the fullest. In this respect, there are many sacrifices and other activities prescribed for those with heavenly aspirations. Most of these recommendations can be found in the karma-kanda section of the Vedas. Karma refers to fruitive activity and kanda means a section or branch. Other religious systems have similar rituals and practices aimed at delivering one to the heavenly planets.

As mentioned before, there is a chief deva, or celestial figure. This is the person most of us refer to as God. Unlike the demigods, however, God has His own planetary system where He resides. Why is this? God has nothing to do with material life. He is above the so-called enjoyment that comes through association with matter. Just as the enjoyment on earth is a reflection of the enjoyment that exists in heaven, the opulences in heaven are simply a reflection of the imperishable riches that exist in the spiritual world where God resides. This reflection isn't complete, but rather it is inverted, or even perverted. The distinction is made because real enjoyment can only come through association with God, who is also known as Lord Krishna. The word Krishna means all-attractive, thus anyone who associates with the all-attractive will surely feel the greatest enjoyment. If we are attracted to something, we will naturally derive some enjoyment out of it. The more attractive something is, the happier it will make us once we associate with it. Since God is the most attractive, it stands to reason that association with Him will give us a feeling of bliss that we've never felt before.

Based on this information, we can conclude that the highest religious practice is that which takes us towards achieving association with the original God. While we can compare the levels of enjoyment on the different planetary systems, there really is no way to quantify the enjoyment felt on the spiritual platform. There is real enjoyment, that which comes through association with Krishna, and false, or illusory, enjoyment. Currently we only know about the illusory enjoyment. We are so illusioned by objects of matter that we think that going to the heavenly planets of the devas will make us happier than we are now. In the eyes of a conditioned entity the demigods certainly do enjoy on a higher level, but even their time there is limited. Eventually everything in this material creation will be destroyed. The same can't be said of God's spiritual world.

So how do we associate with God? We know how to perform sacrifices and offer prayers in hopes of a better condition in life, but how do we take the necessary steps to achieve Krishna's personal association? Thankfully for us, the Lord is kind enough to appear on earth from time to time to show us the way. Not only does He perform transcendental activities for the benefit of others, but His devotees also show us how to properly worship the Lord and please Him to the best of one's ability. One such interaction between God and His devotee took place many thousands of years ago in the forests of India. Lord Krishna, who is also known by His four-handed form of Lord Narayana or Vishnu, came to earth in the form of a handsome and pious prince named Rama. Since Lord Rama is an avatara of Lord Vishnu, He is not different from God. Worship of Rama is worship of God. We living entities, bhutas, are separated expansions of God, so we can't be considered to be on the same level.

Lord Rama performed many wonderful activities during His time on earth. On one occasion, He and His younger brother Lakshmana visited the female sage Shabari. At the time, Rama's wife, Sita Devi, had just been kidnapped, so the Lord was trying to find her whereabouts. Rama was told to visit the sage Shabari, who was residing in the forest and performing great austerities. Shabari's teachers had told her that she would one day achieve salvation by meeting Rama and Lakshmana face to face. In the above referenced quote, Shabari is offering a nice prayer to the Lord after having kindly welcomed the two princes to her hermitage.

This one prayer by Shabari sufficiently describes the meaning of life and how to attain perfection. She kindly addressed Rama as deva vare, which means the chief of the devas. Moreover, she said that she could now easily get to heaven or anywhere else since she had worshiped Rama. Shabari here clearly spells out the difference between Narayana and any other deva, or demigod. Since Nara means man, Narayana is He who is the source of all naras. Since God is the source of all bhutas, or living entities, He is also the source of all enjoyment. By worshiping Rama, one can achieve all the opulences and enjoyment available to those who take up other religious practices.

Since worship of Krishna automatically brings about heavenly opulences and other enjoyments, why would we take to any other type of worship? Not only is Rama the best of the devas, but those who worship Him are the best of the dharmacaris, or those dedicated to religious principles. So how do we perform this worship? It is quite simple actually. We have to show the same level of respect and hospitality towards Lord Rama [God] that Shabari did. Immediately questions may arise as to how we can meet Lord Rama. Sure, Shabari got to welcome Him to her home, but how do we bring Rama into our house? Why would He even agree to come visit us?

The key is to have a desire to associate with God. This desire must be pure and without personal motive. The Lord will already give us what we want, so there is no reason to ask Him for enjoyment or any other kind of pleasure. Shabari simply had a desire to see God, to welcome Him, and to reciprocate the feelings of love that He already had shown her. Shabari hadn't met Rama before, but she knew that God loved her. That love came in the form of her spiritual guides, or gurus. The bona fide spiritual master is a godsend, a person sent from the spiritual world to help us rekindle our forgotten relationship with the Supreme Lord.

So how do we find our guru? How do we receive Krishna's mercy in the form of the gurudeva? If we are sincere in our desires, Krishna will certainly bring us the guru we need. Luckily for us, there are many bona fide spiritual masters that we can easily approach today without having to leave our homes. His Divine Grace A.C. Bhaktivedanta Swami Prabhupada is the foremost teacher of devotional service, or bhakti-yoga, for the people of this age. Though He is no longer present on this planet, His written instructions and recorded words live on. In this way, Shrila Prabhupada never dies.

How do we associate with this great swami? We simply have to follow his instructions, the primary of which calls for the constant chanting of the holy names of God, "Hare Krishna Hare Krishna, Krishna Krishna, Hare Hare, Hare Rama Hare Rama, Rama Rama, Hare Hare", and abstention from the four pillars of sinful life: meat eating, illicit sex, gambling, and intoxication. After we steadily follow these regulations for an extended period of time, we can then take up the process of deity worship. Personal association with God is reserved for the great devotees like Shabari, but it doesn't mean that we are left out in the cold. The deity is the worshipable form of the Lord, hence it is known as the archa vigraha. If we treat the archa-murti with the same love and respect that Shabari showed to Rama, we will most certainly be granted the same benediction of salvation.

CHAPTER 6 - COMPARING RAMAYANAS

"O best of men, today, by worshiping You, Rama who is the greatest of all the gods, my religious practices have become fruitful and my ascension to the heavenly realm will surely take place." (Shabari speaking to Lord Rama, Valmiki Ramayana, Aranya Kand, 74.12)

The Ramayana is one of the most famous literary works in history. More than just a book, it is a wonderful Sanskrit poem which describes the life and pastimes of Lord Shri Rama, a pious prince and celebrated avatara of the Supreme Lord. The Ramayana is so famous that it has sprung many spinoffs and offshoots, other variations of the poem which describe the same events in different levels of detail. Since the Ramayana is so old - old enough that we can't accurately date its composition - it has been studied for centuries. In modern times, scholars, academics, and inquisitive non-devotees have taken to studying the work. They have compared several popular versions and have concluded that the original Ramayana, penned by Maharishi Valmiki, hardly makes any reference at all to Rama being a divine figure, an incarnation of God. Rather, they believe that Rama only became known as a deity many years later. This erroneous conclusion based off mental speculation is refuted many times in the actual text of the Ramayana, including in the section describing the incident where Lord Rama meets the great female sage Shabari.

In order to put things into proper context, familiarity with the nature of some of the other Ramayanas that have come into existence is required. Probably the most famous alternate version, or supplement to Valmiki's Ramayana, is the Ramacharitamanasa, a poem written by Goswami Tulsidas during the sixteenth century. This work is often referred to as the Tulsi Ramayana, but it should be noted that Tulsidas never intended for his work to be taken as the original Ramayana. Rather, he named his book the Ramacharitamanasa, which refers to the mind always contemplating the transcendental activities of Lord Rama. Tulsidas' work is a poem composed in Awadhi, which is a dialect of Hindi. It is funny to see that some scholars have taken up the task to determine whether or not the Ramacharitamanasa is a translation of the original Ramayana. This is humorous because the Ramacharitamanasa was never intended to be a translation, nor has the author claimed that it is one. Rather, it is simply a beautiful poem extolling the virtues of Lord Rama, with a brief summary of His life's activities included.

What was the need for this great work? After all, the Ramayana is one of the holiest scriptures, complete in and of itself. The completeness is what is important in this regard. The Valmiki Ramayana is very long, consisting of thousands of Sanskrit verses. Included are detailed conversations and blow by blow accounts of the fighting that took place between Lord Rama's Vanara army and Ravana's band of Rakshasas. In recent times, several movies have been made of the Ramayana. Obviously the entire work could never be accurately portrayed in a single movie, so each film depicts only a summary of the events. From our personal experience, when we were six years of age, we visited India and through good fortune were exposed to the Ramayana and Lord Rama. When we heard that there were movies made of this Ramayana, we pestered the elders to take us to see one. Our guardians and relatives told us of different Ramayana movies that were in the theaters at the time, but we insisted on seeing whichever one was the longest, which at the time was the Sampoorna Ramayana.

The point of all this is that the Valmiki Ramayana is quite lengthy. Even a movie that claims to be sampurna, or complete, surely isn't. Taking this into consideration, Tulsidas took to writing his own poem about Lord Rama. It should also be noted that we currently live in the age of Kali. This age is known for rampant quarrel and hypocrisy; hence people generally don't have an affinity for spiritual life. Therefore presenting the original Ramayana to society at large is a difficult task. Tulsidas, being a surrendered soul and pure devotee of Lord Rama, wanted to spread the glories of the Lord to everyone, making the pastimes and activities of Rama presentable to a larger audience.

One will notice many differences between the Ramacharitamanasa and the original Ramayana. The narration itself is different, with Tulsidas' version being told from the perspective of a conversation between Lord Shiva and his wife Parvati. This conversation appears in the Brahmanda Purana in a section which is known as the Adhyatma Ramayana, or the spiritual Ramayana. Since this version is from a Purana, its author is Vyasadeva, the great compiler of all the Puranas, Mahabharata, and Vedanta-sutras. The Supreme Lord descends to earth in every creation, but the exact sequence of His activities can vary in each kalpa. The events in the Adhyatma Ramayana are described a little differently, with certain key elements deviating completely from the original. For example, one of the major differences is that the form of Sita, Lord Rama's wife, that is kidnapped by Ravana is only a material version. The Ramacharitamanasa tells us that the real Sita entered the fire just prior to her kidnap, leaving an illusory form for Ravana to take. Upon Ravana's death and Sita's rescue, the original form of Rama's wife reappeared from the fire.

Tulsidas is often criticized for this and other deviations in his work. The harshest critics say that he made his events up, wanting to protect Sita. Lord Chaitanya, Krishna's most recent incarnation to appear on earth, actually corroborated Tulsdias' version of Sita's illusory form being kidnapped. Lord Chaitanya, who roamed the earth prior to Tulsidas' advent, specifically found evidence relating to Sita from the Kurma Purana and showed the original page to a brahmana named Ramadasa Vipra. Ramadasa was a great devotee of Lord Rama and was upset about Sita being kidnapped. Lord Chaitanya, being the original Hari Himself, alleviated the distress of the brahmana by showing him evidence from authorized scripture about the illusory Sita.

The criticisms of Tulsidas are humorous in a sense. Since the saint was so kind and humble, it is understandable that some people would mistake his simple and faithful behavior for lack of intelligence. Yet does anyone seriously believe that Tulsidas didn't know his version was different from the original Ramayana? The saint was a highly learned scholar who had a firm grasp of all Vedic literature, including the Valmiki Ramayana. According to the statements of various saints, Tulsidas is considered to be an incarnation of Valmiki. The Maharishi was disappointed that his original Ramayana failed to properly extol the virtues of Hanuman, thus he decided to come back and praise Rama's devotee to the fullest. Tulsidas did just that by writing the famous Hanuman Chalisa, a devotional poem praising Hanuman which is recited by millions of devotees on a daily basis. In fact, Tulsidas took spiritual instruction from Hanuman and can thus be considered his disciple.

Since Tulsidas' work was so devotional in nature, some scholars declared that Valmiki's version didn't really claim that Rama was an incarnation of God. To give evidence to this fact, they decided that the initial book of the Ramayana, the Bala Kanda, only came into existence later on and that it wasn't part of the original Ramayana. They claimed that the rest of the work never mentions Rama as a divine figure, and that He is depicted to be only a great personality who endured many hardships.

Those making these claims aren't devotees themselves, so they haven't taken in Vedic wisdom from any authority. If one reads Valmiki's Ramayana, there is no doubt that Rama is declared to be God. There are many examples of this, including the time the Lord visited the female sage Shabari. Part of Rama's pastimes involved Him travelling the forests of India as an exile for fourteen years. Rama was of the princely order, and as the eldest son of the king, He was next in line to ascend the throne. Yet due to unfortunate events, Rama was banished from His kingdom for fourteen years. Not able to bear the separation, Rama's wife Sita, and younger brother Lakshmana, insisted on accompanying Him.

Sita was kidnapped by Ravana while the group was living in the forest. During their search for her whereabouts, Rama and Lakshmana came upon the hermitage of Shabari. Upon seeing the two brothers, Shabari immediately got up and touched their feet. This alone is an indication of Rama's divinity. Shabari was a brahmana, or one of the priestly class. Rama and Lakshmana were military men, so they were considered subordinate to Shabari according to social etiquette. Nevertheless, Shabari knew who Rama was and thus treated Him appropriately.

After Rama posed some nice questions to Shabari, the sage responded with some kind words of her own. In the above referenced quote, she refers to Rama as deva vare, which means the chief of the devas, or gods. Deva refers to a demigod, or a celestial being. Similar to the Christian concept of saints, the demigods are the elevated living entities who possess extraordinary power. Those growing up in the Hindu tradition are familiar with the many gods. Outsiders sometimes mistakenly take this to mean that Hindus don't believe in a single God, but this is not the case. The original form of God is Lord Shri Krishna, whose immediate expansion is Lord Narayana, or Vishnu.

There is really no difference between Krishna and Vishnu other than appearance. Krishna has two hands and Narayana has four. The reason for the two forms is that people have different ways of worshiping God. Lord Vishnu is intended to appeal to those who view God with awe and reverence. Is there any other way to view God? Yes. Lord Krishna, being God's original all-attractive form, is meant to attract those who view the Lord with pure love and affection, not caring for His great powers. In this way, we see there are subtle differences between the two forms, but for all intents and purposes, Krishna and Vishnu are the same.

"The highly renowned Rama rages into a fury against those who dare brave against Him. He is extremely powerful, for He can completely stop the onset of a pulsing river simply by using His arrows. Shriman Rama can bring down all the stars, planets, and the sky itself by use of His arrows. He is even capable of saving the earth if it should collapse. The illustrious Rama, if He wanted to, could deluge the whole world by breaking apart the shorelines of the seas. With His arrows, He can resist the onset of the oceans and the wind. After withdrawing the whole world into Himself, that highly renowned best of

men, by virtue of His powers, is capable of again creating the whole world with all its creatures." (Akampana speaking to Ravana, Valmiki Ramayana, Aranya Kand, 31.23-26)

Lord Rama is the chief of the gods because He is an incarnation of Vishnu. Evidence of this is given in the Bala Kanda of the Ramayana, which describes how the demigods approached Lord Vishnu to help them defeat Ravana. The Lord agreed to come to earth as the eldest son of the King of Ayodhya, Maharaja Dasharatha. Evidence of Rama's divinity is also given elsewhere. Akampana, one of Ravana's assistants, personally witnessed Rama's fighting power. The Lord was once attacked by fourteen thousand of Ravana's associates. Rama showed His tremendous prowess by easily killing all the demons. Akampana managed to escape back to Lanka and relay the information to Ravana. In describing the incident, Akampana declared that Rama was capable of swallowing up the entire world and then recreating it with all its creatures. This is a direct reference to Vishnu's ability to create. Brahman is God's feature as the impersonal energy, and it is this energy that the Lord impregnates in order to create life on earth.

Shabari confirms the fact that Rama is Vishnu by stating that He is the greatest of the gods. What does it mean to be the chief god? Demigods can only bestow material rewards. At best, their worshipers can ascend to the heavenly planets, where they remain for some time before returning back to earth. Worshipers of Vishnu, however, aren't looking for any material benefits, and as such, they ascend to the spiritual world after death. The spiritual realm represents an eternal abode, a place where we can check in anytime but never have to leave.

Rama's divinity is not some concoction. Maharishi Valmiki meditated for thousands of years before he took up devotional service and decided to compose the Ramayana. He wouldn't waste his time crafting such a wonderful poem if Rama were just an ordinary human being. We should always try to take in Vedic wisdom from the proper sources. Since Krishna is so attractive, everyone is enamored by Him, even the non-devotees. Yet if someone doesn't have the eyes to see Krishna, they will never be able to properly understand literature which describes Him. Therefore we are advised to learn from devotees. This makes sense because the devotees are Krishna's greatest fans, and as such, they have an eagerness to hear about God. This eagerness results in a desire to study all the great Vedic texts which describe Krishna. Hence devotees know how to take things in their proper context.

The great saints know that people will try to put forth their faulty interpretations of the famous scriptures, so for the benefit of future generations of sincere souls, summary studies and synthesized poetry are written. By consulting works such as the Ramacharitamanasa, we can understand the essence of Krishna and Rama. If an author understands the proper conclusion about life, that of devotional service to God being the highest occupation, their literature will automatically become first class and beneficial to all of society.

CHAPTER 7 - THE IMPERISHABLE REALM

"Those great saints, who are knowers of dharma and greatly fortunate, spoke these words to me: 'Rama will visit your very pious ashrama. Along with Saumitra [Lakshmana], you should offer Rama the greatest hospitality as your guest. Thus after seeing Him, as a benediction, you will ascend to the eternal realm.'" (Shabari speaking to Lord Rama, Valmiki Ramayana, Aranya Kand, 74.15-16)

This one passage from the famous Ramayana succinctly explains the purpose of life. Due to the individuality of the spirit soul, different priorities and philosophies will develop over the course of a lifetime of a living entity. Acting on these desires and aims, individuals take to different activities. One will either succeed or fail in their endeavors, but since none of the objectives are focused on the imperishable, aims and desires will have to be constantly adjusted. For an objective to be considered supreme, it must provide a result which transcends all other results. In the above referenced passage, we are privy to instructions provided by bona fide spiritual guides which aim to produce the highest benefit of life, that of ascension to the imperishable realm, that abode where having gone once, one never returns.

God, the divine creator, the Lord of lords, can assume many shapes and sizes. Since He is so great, some take God to be a man-made creation. This thought process is understandable since the human mind is incapable of conceiving of a perfect entity, someone who is flawless and never falls down. But by carefully studying the workings of this world, we can reach no other conclusion except that which acknowledges God's existence. How do we know this? For starters, let's analyze the terms "flawed" and "temporary". For the concept of fallibility to exist, there must be something which is infallible. If there wasn't something infallible already in existence, then the concept of fallibility would have no meaning. The same holds true with permanence and mutability. We can only understand what "permanent" means by studying things which are not permanent.

Simply based on these facts, we can logically deduce that there must be a single infallible and permanent source for everything that we see in this material world. God is that source, but since the concept of "God" is quite abstract, the authoritative scriptures give us more details about the Supreme. When we say a certain set of scriptures is authoritative, it means that people of authority have declared them to be so. And who are the authority figures? Starting from the time of our birth, the first people we hand control over to is our parents. Next come the spiritual leaders, or gurus. We trust these people because they are in charge of our well-being, and they really have no reason to guide us astray. Should our authority figures happen to be flawed, we can still study the example set by those who are virtuous and well-respected. In any society, there will naturally be a leader or group of people that everyone else follows.

When it comes to understanding God, we must consult spiritual leaders, people who know what they are talking about. The saintly class tells us that God exists and that information about Him can be found in the Vedas, the ancient scriptures of India. The Vedas are the oldest religious books in existence, for one cannot even accurately date their origin. Vedic wisdom was initially passed down through aural reception. This wisdom states that God has many names, forms, and features, even though He is a singular entity.

This divine leader, the Supreme Lord of creation, kindly appears on earth from time to time to help the fallen souls rekindle their forgotten relationship with Him. One such appearance took place many thousands of years ago during the Treta Yuga when Lord Rama, the handsome and pious prince of Ayodhya, roamed the earth. Lord Rama is one of God's most famous incarnations as He is worshiped to this day by millions around the world. Rama especially draws the attention of devotees because, as His name so aptly describes, He gives pleasure to all He comes in contact with. Not only does Rama please by His smile and His nature, but also through His glorious activities.

The activities performed by Rama during His time on earth are so famous that they are chronicled in many Vedic texts. Since Rama appears on earth in every millennium, the exact nature of the events pertaining to His life sometimes differs, but the general sequence is usually the same. The most detailed description of His life and pastimes can be found in the Ramayana, which was compiled by Maharishi Valmiki. The above referenced statement from the Ramayana describes an incident where Rama and His younger brother Lakshmana visited the hermitage of the exalted female sage Shabari.

At the time, Rama and Lakshmana were looking for Rama's wife Sita Devi, who had gone missing. Sita had been kidnapped by the Rakshasa demon Ravana. Lest we think this was a slight on Rama's part, Sita's kidnap was in the cards, part of the great equation that would lead to Ravana's demise. In fact, defeating Ravana was one of the primary reasons for God's advent on earth as a pious and powerful warrior. While roaming the forests looking for Sita, Rama was told to visit Shabari, for the female sage was pious and ever dedicated to performing austerities. Upon approaching the ashrama, Rama and Lakshmana were greeted very kindly by Shabari. The gentle lady kindly touched their feet and welcomed them very hospitably. After exchanging pleasantries, Shabari praised Rama as being the foremost of gods and also told Him of what her spiritual guides had previously told her.

From the statements of Shabari's spiritual guides, we can understand how to achieve perfection in life. In the first part of their instructions, the sages told Shabari to welcome both Rama and Lakshmana hospitably. Hospitality means kindness. This kindness wasn't of the ordinary variety either, for it was to be directed at God and His younger brother. Can God have a brother? Surely He can. Vedic information tells us that God, whose original form is that of Lord Krishna, does not reside in the spiritual world alone. We know from our own lives that we have more fun when our friends and family are with us. In a similar manner, Krishna is the greatest enjoyer, so this means that His enjoyment comes through association with the most exalted souls. These pleasure-givers are a representation of one of Krishna's potencies, namely hladini-shakti. The topmost pleasure-giver to Krishna is Shrimati Radharani, the fountainhead of all goddesses of fortune, or Lakshmis. Sita Devi was in fact an incarnation of Lakshmi, i.e. she was the very same Radha from the spiritual world.

There are different moods, or mellows, through which one can have association with Krishna. Pleasure doesn't always have to come through conjugal love. Krishna also has other associates who give Him pleasure through friendship, fraternity, and parental affection. In this regard, Baladeva, or Lord Balarama, is Krishna's expansion who offers fraternal love and affection. Balarama is actually the embodiment of the spiritual master, God's greatest protector. Just as Rama was an incarnation of Krishna and Sita an incarnation of Radha, Lakshmana was an incarnation of Baladeva.

Shabari was advised to act kindly towards God and His brother. The nature of this kindness is also important to note. Shabari was not advised to simply view Rama and Lakshmana with awe and reverence.

She was not told to respect them because of their great fighting ability or the fact that they were of the princely order. Instead, she was advised to treat Rama and Lakshmana on the same level as she would treat her own family members. After all, the greatest form of hospitality is to treat a fellow stranger on the same level as we would treat a member of our own family. If a relative comes to visit us after a long time, we go to great lengths to make sure they are happy staying in our home. We will clean up the house and whip up the best food preparations in anticipation. The aim of hospitality is to make the guest feel as if they are residing within their own home. This is how Shabari tried to treat Rama and Lakshmana.

The second part of the instructions given to Shabari is a complement to the first part. The first part details what actions are to be taken. The second part deals with the results, the reward Shabari would gain from performing the prescribed set of actions. The nature of this reward is interesting to note. The sages told Shabari that by serving Rama and Lakshmana, she would ascend to a spiritual realm which is imperishable. We should note that Shabari was not told that she would merge into any energy, nor was she told that she would assume a body just like Narayana's. On the contrary, her reward would be ascension to a new home.

For there to be ascension, there has to be movement. But what is actually moving? Is Shabari being carried away to a different location? The ascension in this context refers to the soul. The place we currently inhabit, the material world, is temporary and full of miseries. Not only are our surroundings temporary, but so is the body that we currently occupy. The soul within the body forms the basis of our identity, and thus it is only the soul that remains after our current body is destroyed. It is this soul that moves from one body to the next through the process of transmigration, or what is commonly referred to as reincarnation.

This transmigration process happens automatically; we really have no control over it. However, we do have a say in where the soul will end up next. By studying the instructions given to Shabari, we see that there is a place where the soul can go and never have to return from. If we never return from this place, then it surely must not be part of the material world. After all, the material world is temporary and destined for destruction. If we live in an area forever, then it must exist forever. Not only must this realm always remain in existence, but so must the body that we occupy while living in this place. Hence, we can understand that those who ascend to this spiritual realm must also be given a body which is imperishable.

The spiritual world must be imperishable because for something to be perishable there must also be a place which is never subject to creation or destruction. The authorized scriptures such as the Bhagavad-gita and Shrimad Bhagavatam inform us that this ever-existing realm is known as the spiritual world. This shouldn't be confused with the concept of heaven. Heaven is a place of elevated sense pleasure, a place which allows for enjoyment on a higher level than we are currently accustomed to. The heavenly planets are also considered to be part of the perishable world; so ascension to this realm cannot be considered the highest achievement in life.

The Vedanta-sutras state that everything in this world emanates from the Absolute Truth, or God. The variegatedness of this world is simply a reflection of those things found in Krishna's realm. If something is considered a reflection, it means that the real thing must exist somewhere. If the real object didn't exist, there would be no meaning to the concept of reflection.

The instructions given by the sages to Shabari actually apply to every single person in this world. Though Rama and Lakshmana aren't roaming the earth today in their original forms, they have kindly incarnated in the form of a transcendental sound vibration. This vibration is known as the maha-mantra, "Hare Krishna Hare Krishna, Krishna Krishna, Hare Hare, Hare Rama Hare Rama, Rama Rama, Hare Hare". Anyone who treats this mantra with love and respect, who honors this sacred formula by regularly chanting it, will surely receive the same benedictions that were bestowed upon Shabari. This is the magic of devotional service. We should all welcome God into our homes by reciting His name, worshiping His deity, and always remembering His glorious pastimes.

CHAPTER 8 - FRUITS OF THE FOREST

"O best among men, thus I was spoken to at that time by those greatly fortunate sages. O best among men, indeed for Your sake I have collected a variety of forest fruits which were growing on the banks of the Pampa Lake, O tiger among men." (Shabari speaking to Lord Rama, Valmiki Ramayana, Aranya Kand, 74.17)

For those new to Vedic traditions, one of the first noticeable practices is the reverence shown to the spiritual master, or guru. We may be accustomed to worshiping God in our minds and offering Him our prayers, but followers of the Vedic tradition offer dandavats when approaching exalted personalities. Dandavats refers to falling on the ground like a rod, or danda, and it is the greatest sign of humility. This obeisance is offered not only in the presence of the guru, but also in the temple to the deity and to pictures of the guru. This style of surrender may seem off-putting to some, but it has a unique purpose. The spiritual master is the via-medium, the boatman who can rescue us from the ocean of misery. The guru has seen the light, and he is kind enough to show others what he has learned. His instructions are actually quite simple, but following through on them without reservation is not.

Since we are born ignorant and helpless, we have all followed the instructions of someone at some point in our lives. Parents guide us through the early years, so they usually remain our primary source of knowledge and instruction. The mother-daughter relationship is certainly unique. Fathers love to spend time with their sons and maybe pass along some words of advice, but the mothers take the role of teacher much more seriously when it comes to their daughters. Any good parent wants to one day marry off their daughter to a nice family, finding a husband who matches well with the daughter's needs and desires. Once the girl leaves the family, she is technically on her own, so it is important that she be imbibed with the fundamentals of life and good values in her youth.

In the Vedic tradition, mothers teach their daughters how to survive in a marriage. Marriage is known as a religious institution, the grihastha ashrama. The husband and wife are to live together for the purpose of cultivating spiritual knowledge. It's uncommon to find both the husband and wife dedicated to spirituality, so usually the burden falls upon only one of them. In modern times, it is common to see the women take charge of the day-to-day religious duties relating to the family. The wives make sure to perform arati [the offering of a lamp in front of the deity] in the home at least twice a day, offering and distributing prasadam at the same time. The deity shouldn't be mistaken to be an idol. God is one, so He is the Supreme Lord for every single living entity in this world. Since we don't have the eyes to see Him in our conditioned state, the Lord is kind enough to take other forms that are more conducive for worship. A person's identity doesn't change throughout their lifetime, but we see that we treat them differently depending on their current body. We treat a young child much differently than we treat an elderly person. We like to hold babies, kiss them, and make funny faces at them. We wouldn't dare repeat the same behavior with the same children when they become adults. Therefore we can conclude that the childhood form of the living entity is the one most conducive for the offering of love.

In a similar manner, God is Absolute, but He takes certain forms that make it easier for the living entities to offer worship. The deity is an incarnation of God known as the archa-vigraha, or worshipable body. Deity worship can involve large statues and elaborate rituals, but it can also be very simple. In a typical Vaishnava family, one will find an altar set up somewhere in the home to allow family members to offer worship.

The women usually take charge of this process inside of family life. But where do they learn the correct procedures and prayers to be used in such worship? Where do they learn how to prepare the proper offerings such as ghee and panchamrita? Where do they learn the sacred formulas to chant? This information is taught to young girls by their mothers. When these girls get married and eventually have their own daughters, they then pass down the same information. In this way, we see that the women of the Vedic tradition have their own parampara, or disciplic succession.

Mothers teaching their daughters is but one example of the guru-disciple relationship. This system only works when there is humble submission. What's interesting to note is that the instructions given are usually quite simple. A good teacher will stick to a few key points and focus on them. The disciple in this relationship doesn't have to be a close friend, family member, or one of a higher caste. It can be anyone who is in need of help. The guru is willing to help anyone who is sincerely interested in reforming themselves. An example of this mercy was seen with the great Narada Muni a long long time ago. The Vedas tell us that the bona fide spiritual master is one who is completely devoted to Lord Krishna, or God. This means that they are free from all other defects and desires. Sometimes someone will seriously take up religious life, but since they have accumulated so many attachments from their material life, their devotional life will be mixed. They may enjoy worshiping God, but at the same time, they'll have other material causes they will spend their time on. The best spiritual master is one who has completely given up all hopes of happiness in material life. Krishna is one who is all-attractive, thus His devotees receive all the happiness they need through associating with Him. Since Krishna provides the highest form of happiness, devotees have no reason to look for happiness anywhere else.

What's so wonderful about Krishna's adherents is that they are not misers. They are liberated souls, but they are not content with just having Krishna for themselves. They know the Truth, so they are not afraid to tell it to others, especially those who are trapped in a miserable condition. Narada Muni is one of the most famous gurus in history. His disciples are the who's who of transcendentalists. On one occasion, Narada was wandering through a forest when he saw a bunch of animals half-killed. They had been shot by a hunter and were on the verge of death. Narada approached the hunter and asked him why he was engaged in such abominable activity. "Either leave the animals alone or just kill them outright. Why are you letting them suffer?" The hunter replied that he was deriving enjoyment from this half-killing and that this was the way he was taught to hunt from his childhood.

Long story short, Narada advised the hunter to give up killing for a living and instead take to worship of Tulasi Devi, the sacred plant and beloved maidservant of Krishna. The hunter was a little worried though. If he gave up hunting and simply took to worshiping a plant, how would he eat? How would he survive? Narada told the hunter not to worry about it; that he would take care of all the arrangements. How kind is Narada Muni? Since the time of our youth, we are taught all these lessons in life about how to do things the right way and how we should be self-sufficient, but Narada didn't discuss any of these details. He told the hunter to simply worship Tulasi Devi and not worry about anything else.

The hunter took his advice and, to his surprise, people came to see him, offering large quantities of food as a gift. Narada Muni had told the neighboring residents that a saintly man had come to the forest and was taking up worship of Tulasi Devi. The residents wanted to show respect to such a person, so they brought him more than enough food. And what was the result of this change in lifestyle? The hunter soon became so kindhearted that he would hop around instead of just walking. He didn't want to hurt a single ant on the ground. This shows the true power of a spiritual master. Following their simple instructions, one can go from being a ruthless hunter to the most harmless person.

Many thousands of years ago, Lord Krishna incarnated on earth as a handsome prince named Rama. During one period in His life, the Lord was roaming the forests with His younger brother Lakshmana. At the time, a great female sage by the name of Shabari was also residing in the forest. As mentioned before, women in the Vedic tradition are usually trained up to be devoted wives, caretakers of the family. Shabari, however, was an ascetic, so she transcended all the rules and regulations of material life. She was dedicated to asceticism, and as a reward, her spiritual guides gave her instructions on how to achieve liberation from the cycle of birth and death. They told her that Lord Rama was coming to visit her soon and that she should welcome Him hospitably and offer Him nice food to eat.

In the above referenced statement, Shabari is explaining what her gurus taught her and how she was following their advice. We should take note of the type of offering she made to Rama, that of fruits and berries of the forest. Living the life of a brahmana, Shabari was non-violent by nature and also renounced, so she had no possessions. In this case, what could she offer God? Based on the results of her action, we can see that her offering to Rama was first class. Lord Rama was greatly pleased with her hospitality, and He granted her liberation from the cycle of birth and death as a reward. Shabari ascended to the imperishable spiritual planets after meeting Rama.

How was Lord Rama satisfied with some wild fruits? After all, Rama and Lakshmana were of the royal order, which was known to eat meat from time to time. God transcends any and all material designations, but when He comes to earth, He plays the part of a person belonging to a specific class of society. Rama and Lakshmana were members of the kshatriya caste, i.e. they were warriors and administrators by trade. In those times, kshatriyas were allowed to kill certain animals as a way of practicing their fighting skills. As a result, they also ate meat from time to time. We shouldn't mistake this type of meat eating with the modern day practice of slaughterhouses. All the animals killed by Rama and Lakshmana were offered up in a religious sacrifice prior to eating. This means that the souls of the animals were promoted to a higher species in the next life.

Though the warrior caste sometimes ate meat, we see that Shabari's spiritual guides didn't advise her to kill any animals. On the contrary, they told her to gather whatever she could and then offer it with love and devotion. This is the most important factor in religious life. God is the most fortunate; He has all the wealth in the world. So what need does He have for our wealth? He's not looking for quantity, but quality. Offering whatever we have at our disposal with love and devotion is enough to make the Lord happy.

Lord Chaitanya gave all the people of this age the simplest formula for achieving success in spiritual life. He advised everyone to simply chant, "Hare Krishna Hare Krishna, Krishna Krishna, Hare Hare, Hare Rama Hare Rama, Rama Rama, Hare Hare", as often as possible. Lord Chaitanya was a perfect spiritual master and, being an incarnation of Krishna, He also empowered future generations of disciples to offer spiritual guidance to mankind. Anyone can follow this simple formula of chanting God's names and eating Krishna prasadam. There is no loss on our part, and as we saw with the examples of the hunter and Shabari, by following the guru's instructions, all other issues in life are taken care of automatically.

CHAPTER 9 - LOST IN IGNORANCE

"O best among men, thus I was spoken to at that time by those greatly fortunate sages. O best among men, indeed for Your sake I have collected a variety of forest fruits which were growing on the banks of the Pampa Lake, O tiger among men." (Shabari speaking to Lord Rama, Valmiki Ramayana, Aranya Kand, 74.17)

All individual souls are equal in their constitutional position. Similar to how we are advised to not judge a book by its cover, the outer dress of the spirit soul is misleading with respect to identification and attribute possession. The spirit soul – an entity which is anatomically independent and yet dependent on the divine will at the same time - forms the basis of identity in all forms of life. This soul is so amazing that its presence can only be realized through outwards symptoms such as the movements and growth cycles of material bodies. The presence of the soul is best exhibited during the events of birth and death, wherein the soul respectively enters and exits its temporary apartment. Once this dwelling is entered, it starts to grow and leave byproducts. Upon the exit of the soul from the dwelling, the same body immediately starts to decay. Therefore it can be concluded that the soul itself is the master of the house, the guiding force behind the changes we see around us.

Though the soul is powerful and naturally knowledgeable, when it gets placed into one of these temporary homes, its natural splendor is hidden. This is similar to how darkness prevails over the land when the sun sets. The sun really hasn't gone anywhere, for the earth's rotation has caused it to be temporarily taken out of sight. Darkness is simply the absence of light, the covering up of the immense spark known as the sun. When the soul is covered up by material elements, the natural propensity for knowledge is similarly shrouded, with the most obvious indication of this cloak being the false identification that is adopted by the majority of the conditioned souls. This false identification can take many forms but it begins with the use of the terms "I" and "Mine". "I" is taken to be the body, and anything it interacts with and enjoys is considered to be "Mine". In reality, these external objects are merely manifestations of material elements, those created by divine beings. The soul has no more possession of these objects than does the matter itself, which is by constitution lifeless and incapable of action. One may own a particular car, but it would be silly to say that the person is the car. Saying that "I am the car" is as silly as the car saying "I am you." Yet this is precisely what occurs with the false identifications that manifest through the practices of nationalism, racism, and sectarianism.

In its constitutional position, the soul is a lover of God. The spiritual spark is simply an emanation from the original source of energy that is God. Since the energy and the energetic are linked in terms of makeup, there is an inherent relationship between the two entities. Naturally the more powerful entity will take on a prominent role in the relationship, with the inferior entity offering its service and loving sentiments. This isn't to say that either party is superior in the grand scheme of things, for if both parties adhere to their roles, there is oneness in the emotions that are exchanged. The energetic party, represented by God, never changes its makeup, but the energy expansions have a choice in where they reside. When the consciousness of the spiritual spark is pure, the individual remains in the company of the energetic and thus takes part in the bliss experienced through sharanagati, or complete surrender. When the individual instead takes to pleasing itself, the connection with the Divine Being is broken, and the soul is cast off into a temporary realm where knowledge of its relationship to its eternal lover is forgotten.

Dharma, or religiosity, is instituted in the temporary realm as a way to allow the wayward soul to reassume its natural position in the spiritual sky as servitor of the Supreme. Abiding by dharma is not easy, so steadfast dedication to rules and regulations, along with adherence to the practice of bhakti-yoga, or devotional service, is required. The highest dharma, or system of religion, is a discipline involving positive and negative activities, with the restricted activities often receiving more attention than the assertive ones. The positive activities of devotional service involve hearing, remembering, worshiping, and surrendering unto the lotus feet of the Lord, who appears in the temporary world in various non-different forms. Of all His forms that are perceptible to the conditioned entity, none is more powerful than the sound vibration representation.

This audible form can be regularly created and honored by chanting, "Hare Krishna Hare Krishna, Krishna Krishna, Hare Hare, Hare Rama Hare Rama, Rama Rama, Hare Hare"

The assertive aspects of devotional service are quite harmless and easy to follow, but the restrictive actions are more likely to be the subject of controversy. Though there are a variety of sins and restricted activities, the Vedic seers have highlighted the four most dangerous ones: meat eating, gambling, illicit sex, and intoxication. These four activities stand out above all the rest because they prove to be the most effective at maintaining the cloud of ignorance that envelops the conditioned soul. Every living entity possesses the same level of knowledge and love for the Supreme Lord. But in the conditioned state, there are differences in the density levels of the clouds that surround the soul. The path to liberation is found through taking to activities which help remove this cloud of ignorance. The four pillars of sinful life are the most dangerous because they help increase one's ignorance, and thus keep the individual firmly grounded in material life. One's stay in the temporary realm doesn't end with the death of the body or the destruction of the universe. Reentry into the spiritual world is not so simple. The conditioned living entity remains separated from its divine lover for as long as it desires to. If this desire remains at the time of death, the spirit soul is again cast into the ocean of nescience, wherein they are again given a temporary body which clouds their natural intelligence.

The sincere souls will gradually make progress in their spiritual pursuits, taking to various aspects of devotional service and making a good-faith effort to refrain from the most sinful of activities. There are others, however, who are so clouded in ignorance that not only will they shun devotional service, but they will actively seek to thwart the activities of those who are trying to return to the spiritual world. Attacking the positive activities of devotional service is a little difficult to do, as they are harmless in and of themselves. How can one argue against chanting and dancing in transcendental ecstasy when similar activities are already adopted by the non-devotees? No, the asuras, the demoniac non-devotees, will focus their criticisms on the restrictive aspects of devotional service, especially that of no meat eating.

Those who are unfamiliar with Vedic traditions will certainly find the restriction on meat eating a little strange at first. Anytime we encounter a new tradition or way of life, we are sure to find it odd. Many people who take to devotional service are actually so enamored by the restriction on meat eating that they will divert their attention towards advancing the cause of vegetarianism. While it is certainly noble to lead the crusade against the practice of unnecessary animal killing, it should be noted that the constitutional position of the soul and its relationship with the Supreme Lord have nothing to do with any positive and negative activities, or the piety and sin related to any action. Rather, the soul's nature is to be a lover of God, so any activity which can maintain this bond of affection, and which at the same time doesn't deviate from the Lord's wishes, is deemed worthy of adopting.

The restriction on meat eating is simple enough to understand. Since every individual is a soul at the core, all forms of life must be treated with respect and love. This includes the animals. A cow or a chicken may not be as intelligent as a human being, but it still eats, sleeps, mates, and defends. It has a spirit soul inside of it, and it is simply going through its life cycle of karma, gradually ascending to the human species. Only the human being is capable of understanding the soul, dharma, and bhakti. When an animal is killed unnecessarily simply for the satisfaction of the taste buds of the killer, the activity certainly can't be considered a religious one. Not only is the natural progress of the animal checked, but the laws of karma will force the killer to suffer in the future. While a government may be lax in its administration of justice and fairness, karma spares no one. It is completely fair and just, so if we kill another entity without cause, we will surely suffer the same fate in the future. In addition, eating meat keeps one attached to the sense demands brought forth by the taste buds. If this attachment remains at the time of death, liberation cannot be achieved.

The asuras, those who don't believe in a soul or a God, have no problem eating meat. They think that everything begins and ends with the current life, so the natural occupation is to try to enjoy the senses as much as possible. Luckily, this line of thinking, which is completely rooted in ignorance, doesn't resonate well with others. But the asuras are not so faint of heart; they have a deep attachment to their sinful way of life. In order to convince others of their ways, the asuras will take to criticizing the Vedic traditions and the various incarnations of Godhead who have appeared on earth. One area of criticism focuses on meat eating, wherein the asuras claim that Shri Rama, a famous incarnation of the original Divine Being, roamed this earth and killed many innocent animals and then ate them. Raising this apparent contradiction, the asuras hope to convince others that Rama cannot be God and that meat eating is certainly not a problem. It is not uncommon to find such persons at social gatherings, where wanton talk of all subjects flows very freely. Such people, who are usually unabashed smokers, drinkers, and meat eaters, hold much anger and resentment towards Shri Rama, Lord Brahma, and other popular figures of the Vedic tradition. Their criticisms directed at worshipable divine figures certainly can dishearten those devotees who are not familiar with the full breadth of Vedic instruction. This is precisely the intention of the asuras, for they themselves are lost in a sea of ignorance, and instead of trying to elevate themselves to safety, they would rather take everyone else down with them.

Lord Rama appeared on this earth many thousands of years ago during the Treta Yuga in the guise of a warrior prince, one of the kshatriya order. During His time, pious kings would regularly perform grand sacrifices as a way of blessing their kingdom and its inhabitants. Many of these sacrifices involved the killing of animals. This shouldn't be mistaken to mean that the kings were avid meat eaters or that they were attached to violence. These animal sacrifices were religious functions, wherein the souls of the animals would automatically be promoted to a higher species in the next life. The kings were also in charge of protecting the innocent, so they had to be expert fighters. In order to become an expert bow warrior, one has to regularly practice. This practice came in the form of hunting, wherein deer and other animals were killed in the forest and then offered up as sacrifice. Again, there was no sense gratification involved in such activity.

There is some controversy as to whether or not Lord Rama and His three younger brothers ate meat or not. From the Valmiki Ramayana, the original composition describing the life and pastimes of Shri Rama, we see that the Lord on several occasions had to shoot deer in the forest. One of the most notable time periods of Rama's life was His fourteen year exile in the forest, where He had to live as a recluse with no claim to the regal life. Prior to leaving, Rama made mention of the fact that He would have to live without eating nice food, including meat. Taking His younger brother Lakshmana and wife Sita Devi with Him, Rama embarked on His journey. Early on, the group created a cottage in an area pointed out to them by the sage Bharadvaja. Prior to entering this newly erected cottage, Lakshmana went out and shot an antelope with an arrow. The antelope's meat was then cooked and offered up to various demigods [celestials in heaven in charge of various departments of material nature] so that they would bless the new establishment. Later on in their journey, Rama and Lakshmana met a Rakshasa named Kabandha, who advised the brothers to visit a lake called Pampa. In describing the lake, the Rakshasa said that there would be many wonderful fish in the lake for Lakshmana to take and offer up to Rama.

Based on these descriptions, it would be reasonable enough to assume that Rama and Lakshmana ate meat from time to time. They were after all members of the royal order, so they certainly took part in many sacrifices. Reasonable arguments can also be made supporting the contrary opinion which states that there is no evidence of Rama ever actually eating meat. When He visited the Nishada chief Guha in the forest, Rama was offered every nice type of food and drink available, but He declined to take part in them due to His vow of asceticism. There is also another incident where Shri Hanuman, the eternal servant of Rama, mentions that the Lord had not reduced Himself to drinking liquor or eating animal flesh while residing in the forest.

"Raghava [Rama] is not enjoying animal flesh, nor even giving service to liquor. He always eats in the evening whatever food has been well provided by the forest." (Hanuman speaking to Sita Devi, Valmiki Ramayana, Sundara Kand, 36.41)

In either case, there is no duplicity on the Lord's part. Even if Rama did eat meat, there is no violation of the rules against violence towards animals or the eating of animal flesh. God is the object of dharma, the ultimate reservoir of pleasure. Dharma is the set of law codes instituted to allow a person to purify their consciousness. The laws themselves are not the objects of pleasure or ultimate destination. Dharma is simply a guideline for how to do something properly. Just as there are included instruction manuals advising one how to construct an exercise machine or piece of office furniture, dharma provides a how-to guide for spiritual success. Yet the knower of God has no need for the instruction manual; they are already connected with Supreme Spirit. If the pure devotee transcends all rules and regulations of dharma, surely the Supreme Lord must as well.

In addition to refraining from eating meat, devotees are advised to offer food in the mode of goodness to Shri Krishna, the original form of Godhead, or one of His non-different expansions, and eat the remnants of the offered food. These remnants are known as prasadam, which means the Lord's mercy. It should be noted that Krishna does not accept any meat items. Even during His time on earth as Lord Rama, God never accepted meat offerings from anyone. When He visited the female sage Shabari, Rama accepted the nice berries and fruits offered to Him. The grand animal sacrifices that were performed were all for the benefit of various demigods, celestial figures who are not as powerful as God. A demigod can be thought of as a government minister, a representative of the chief. The representative isn't the same in power or stature as the chief, and they only concentrate their efforts on various workings of the government. The demigods are in charge of things like weather, good fortune, bad fortune, and illness. Sacrificed animals were never offered to Lord Krishna or His direct expansion of Lord Vishnu.

The asuras, nevertheless, will continue to point to Rama's activities involving the killing of animals as a sign of contradiction. While these non-devotees are enamored by Rama's violent activities, they completely ignore all of the Lord's other features and qualities. If the asuras want to imitate Rama's purported meat eating, why not imitate His benevolent behavior towards brahmanas and other pious entities? Why don't the asuras try to take on 14,000 of the most powerful miscreants in the world and come out successful? Why don't they remain steadfast to dharma and the injunctions of the Vedas? Why don't they honor their mother and father in every possible way? Why don't they renounce all opulences and amenities in favor of serving parents and elders? Why don't they imitate Rama's equal disposition towards all the citizens that lived in His kingdom of Ayodhya? Why don't they imitate His behavior towards exalted sages such as Valmiki, Bharadvaja, Agastya, and Atri, wherein the Lord prostrated Himself before them and offered to serve them with every fiber of His being?

Maya, the illusory energy pervading the material world, is certainly a cruel mistress. The demoniac are the most scorned of lovers, for their loveable object is illusion. Unable to derive any happiness from unrequited love, the asuras take to criticizing those who have found the only source of pleasure in both the material and spiritual worlds. The demons will always try to create dissension by raising doubts in the minds of the pure-hearted devotees. The asuras are slaves to illusion, so naturally they will concoct unfounded theories and ideas about Shri Krishna and His various avataras. Yet just as the evil elements headed by the demon Ravana were defeated by Shri Rama and His sincere Vanara servants, the demons of today can be quickly cast aside by regularly remembering the lotus feet of the Supreme Lord and His powerful emissaries like Hanuman.

ABOUT THE AUTHOR

The author, Sonal Pathak, can be contacted through email: **info@krishnasmercy.org**

Other Krishna's Mercy titles from the same author:
Lifter of Mountains
Forever Rama's
Devoted to Rama
Lord Rama: The Shelter for the Saints
Meeting Hanuman
Subduer of Enemies
Caught Butter Handed
How We Met: Sita Describing Her Marriage to Rama
Questions About Krishna
The Sharpest Knife: Lakshmana and His Words of Wisdom

Printed in Great Britain
by Amazon